Alexander Graham Bell

By Wil Mara

Consultants
Nanci R. Vargus, Ed.D.
Primary Multiage Teacher
Decatur Township Schools, Indianapolis, Indiana

Katharine A. Kane, Reading Specialist
Former Language Arts Coordinator
San Diego County Office of Education

Children's Press ®
A Division of Scholastic Inc.
New York   Toronto   London   Auckland   Sydney
Mexico City   New Delhi   Hong Kong
Danbury, Connecticut

Designer: Herman Adler Design
Photo Researcher: Caroline Anderson
The photo on the cover shows Alexander Graham Bell.

Library of Congress Cataloging-in-Publication Data

Mara, Wil.
   Alexander Graham Bell / by Wil Mara.
     p. cm. — (Rookie biographies)
Includes Index.
Summary: A brief introduction to the life of the man who
invented the telephone.
    ISBN 0-516-22524-3 (lib. bdg.)   0-516-27340-X (pbk.)
    1. Bell, Alexander Graham, 1847-1922—Juvenile literature.
2. Inventors—United States—Biography—Juvenile literature.
3. Telephone—History. [1. Bell, Alexander Graham, 1847-1922.
2. Inventors. 3. Telephone—History.] I. Title. II. Rookie biography.
    TK6143.B4 M367 2002
    621.385'092—dc21   2002008773

Did you know Alexander
Graham Bell invented
the telephone?

Bell was born in the country of Scotland on March 3, 1847. He was interested in communication.

Communicating is when you
pass an idea from one person
to another. When you talk,
you are communicating.

Bell's father and grandfather taught deaf people. A deaf person is someone who cannot hear.

The Bells taught their students
how to shape their mouths so
they could speak more clearly.

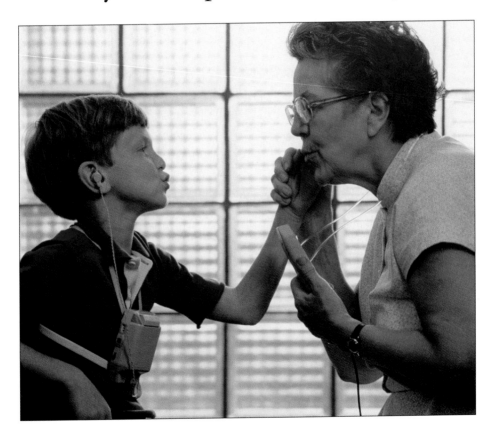

Alexander Graham Bell also helped teach the deaf. He is shown here at a school for the deaf. Bell is located at the top right of this picture.

9

In Bell's time, people who lived far away used a telegraph to communicate. A telegraph was a small machine with a button that you tapped with your finger. It sent simple sounds, like beeps, to other places over a wire.

11

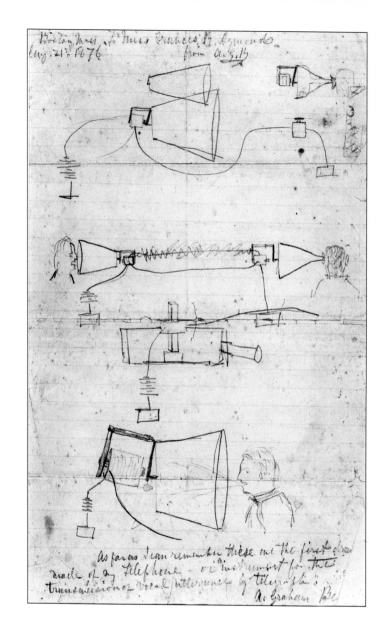

Boston Mass.   for Miss Frances E. Symonds
Aug. 21st 1876   from A. G. B.

As far as I can remember these are the first drawings
made of my Telephone — or instrument for the
transmission of vocal utterances by telegraph."
A. Graham Bell

Bell believed there was a way
to send the sound of a person's
voice over a wire to other places.
He needed help with this idea.

In 1874 he met a man named
Thomas Watson. Watson was
very good at building things.
Bell and Watson spent many
months trying to build a
machine that could send
voice sounds.

16

On March 10, 1876, Bell spilled something on his clothes. He yelled for Watson to come help him. Watson was in another room. He heard Bell through their machine. This was the first telephone call!

At first a lot of people thought Bell's invention was some kind of trick. So, in 1877, Bell showed groups of people how the telephone worked.

BOSTON

SALEM

THE TELEPHONE

19

By 1892, a telephone wire was set up between the cities of New York and Chicago. Bell spoke through a phone in New York to officially mark the beginning of long distance phone service.

Bell did many other things after he invented the telephone. He went back to working with deaf children.

24

He also helped start the National Geographic Society. This society is still around today!

You can find Bell in the front row on the far right in this picture.

Bell died on August 2, 1922.
He was 75 years old.

What would your life be like without the telephone? It would be hard to talk to people who live far away. Remember the hard work of Alexander Graham Bell the next time you use the telephone.

Words You Know

Alexander Graham Bell

communication

deaf

National Geographic Society

30

school

telegraph

telephone

Thomas Watson

Index

About the Author

Wil Mara has written over fifty books. His works include both fiction and nonfiction for children and adults. He lives with his wife and three daughters in northern New Jersey.

Photo Credits

Photographs © 2002: Alexander Graham Bell National Historic Site of Canada/ Parks Canada: 6, 9, 23, 27, 30 top left, 31 top left; Brown Brothers: 4, 16, 19; Corbis Images: 7, 30 bottom left (Nathan Benn), 28, 31 bottom left (Laura Dwight), 24, 30 bottom right (Underwood & Underwood), 5, 30 top right (Jennie Woodcock/ Reflections Photolibrary), 3, 15, 31 bottom right; Library of Congress: 12; North Wind Picture Archives: 11, 20, 31 top right; Superstock, Inc.: cover.